A Faithful Life

THE STORY OF JOSEPH SMITH IN PICTURES

GLEN S. HOPKINSON

DESERET BOOK
SALT LAKE CITY, UTAH

Library of Congress Cataloging-in-Publication Data
Hopkinson, Glen S., 1946–
    A faithful life : the story of Joseph Smith in pictures / Glen S. Hopkinson.
      p. cm.
    Includes bibliographical references.
    ISBN 1-59038-350-8 (hardbound : alk. paper)
    1. Smith, Joseph, 1805-1844—Art. 2. Mormons—Biography—Art. 3. Church of Jesus Christ of Latter-day Saints—Biography—Art. 4. Mormon Church—Biography—Art. I. Title.
    BX8695.S6H67 2005
    289.3'092—dc22
      2004019026

Printed in China   18961
R. R. Donnelley and Sons, Schenzhen, China

10   9   8   7   6   5   4   3   2   1

Yea, Joseph [son of Jacob] truly said: Thus saith the Lord unto me: A choice seer will I raise up out of the fruit of thy loins. . . .

And unto him will I give power to bring forth my word . . . unto the confounding of false doctrines and laying down of contentions, and establishing peace. . . .

And out of weakness he shall be made strong. . . .

And thus prophesied Joseph, saying: Behold, that seer will the Lord bless. . . .

And his name shall be called after me; and it shall be after the name of his father. And . . . [that] which the Lord shall bring forth by his hand, by the power of the Lord shall bring my people unto salvation (2 Nephi 3:7, 11–15).

"It has been borne in upon my soul that one of my descendants will promulgate a work to revolutionize the world of religious faith."

—ASAEL SMITH, GRANDFATHER OF JOSEPH SMITH JR.

Joseph Smith was born in a farmhouse in Vermont in December 1805.

The Smith Family

Sometimes the greatest events happen quietly.

Joseph Smith, the prophet of the Restoration, was born in a humble farmhouse in Sharon, Vermont, on December 23, 1805. His father was a farmer named Joseph Smith. His mother was named Lucy. He had two older brothers (seven-year-old Alvin and five-year-old Hyrum) and one sister (two-year-old Sophronia). He was named Joseph after his father.

The Smiths were a loving, close-knit family. Father Joseph and Mother Lucy raised their children to pray and read the Bible. Occasionally some of the children were able to attend school, but most of the time they had duties to fill on the farm.

In 1812 and 1813, an epidemic of typhoid fever swept through the area, leaving thousands dead.

All of the Smith children became ill, and some nearly died. Seven-year-old Joseph began to recover, but then suffered a severe pain in his leg. His mother wrote: "His leg immediately began to swell and he continued in the most excruciating pain for two weeks longer. . . . I carried him in my arms nearly continually, soothing him and doing all that . . . [I] could to ease his suffering, until . . . I was taken severely ill myself.

"Then Hyrum, who was always remarkable for his tenderness and sympathy, desired that he might take my place. . . . Hyrum sat beside him almost incessantly day and night, grasping the most painful part of the affected leg between his hands and, by pressing it closely, enabled the little sufferer the better to bear the pain which otherwise seemed almost ready to take his life."

A local surgeon said Joseph's leg needed to be removed. But another surgeon from nearby Dartmouth College agreed to try a new procedure to try to save the leg. Joseph showed great courage during the operation. He refused to be tied down by cords, and he refused the whiskey the doctor offered as an anesthetic. He asked instead that his father hold him in his arms. The suffering was intense, but the surgery was a success. Joseph had to use crutches for three years and walked with a slight limp throughout his life.

When Joseph's leg was infected, Hyrum squeezed it to help ease the pain.

In April 1815, Joseph Sr. and Lucy Smith were farming and raising their large family of seven children in Norwich, Vermont. They were beginning what would become the second season of drought, resulting in vast crop failures.

That same month, half a world away, Mt. Tambora on the island of Sumbawa in Indonesia erupted, exploding in tremendous violence and fury that the world seldom sees.

The volcano sent dust and ash miles into the earth's atmosphere, obscuring the sun. Seasons were affected around the world. The next year in Vermont, and in many other places in the northern hemisphere, was known as "The Year without Summer." Snow fell in June. Killing frosts came in July and then again in August.

The family worked hard, but nothing they did could overcome the near famine caused by the unusual weather. Father Smith decided they had to move to New York, where land was cheap.

In the fall of 1816 Father Smith left for Palmyra, New York, and he later sent a wagon for his family to follow. Mother Lucy and her eight children (including one born in March) made the difficult 300-mile journey through the snow and cold of November.

The eruption of Mt. Tambora in Indonesia brought snow to Vermont the following summer.

I arrived in Palmyra with a small portion of my effects, my babes, and two cents in money. . . . The joy I felt in throwing myself and my children upon the care and affection of a tender husband and father doubly paid me for all I had suffered. The children surrounded their father, clinging to his neck, covering his face with tears and kisses that were heartily reciprocated by him."

—LUCY MACK SMITH

The Smith family moved from Vermont to Palmyra, New York.

When the Smiths moved to Palmyra, they planned together how to purchase new land.

When they arrived in Palmyra, as Lucy recorded, "We all now sat down and maturely counseled together as to what course it was best to take, and how we should proceed . . . in our then destitute circumstances."

They agreed that Joseph Sr. and the two oldest sons would find work to pay for 100 acres of land. Meanwhile, Lucy was able to keep food in the house by painting and selling oilcloth coverings for tables.

Farming was back-breaking, gut-wrenching work. Joseph Sr. and his two older boys cleared trees and rocks. They plowed, furrowed, planted, and then reaped what they could.

They fed and cared for the animals, as well as butchered the hogs, chickens, steers, and sheep as the need arose. They also hunted for large and small game for the kitchen table.

Thirteen-year-old Sophronia was a great help to her mother in doing the chores that women did on the farms. She washed, sewed, mended, cooked, and tended the baby and the little boys.

Joseph Jr. was still somewhat lame from the terrible operation three years earlier. Still, work was required. He could hitch and drive the team, chop wood and slop the hogs, as well as teach his younger brothers to milk the cows, gather eggs, and harvest the fruits and vegetables.

All family members, even little children, were extremely important members of the "work force" on the farm in the early nineteenth century. Children began with the more simple chores, such as gathering eggs, weeding the garden, shelling corn. Later they would learn to milk the cows, slop the hogs, and feed the animals. Young girls would work along with their mother and sisters in washing, sewing, mending, and cooking. The boys would work in the fields with their fathers.

Even though they were nearly six years apart in age, Joseph
and Hyrum grew to be extremely close. As John Taylor
wrote later, "In life they were not divided, and in death
they were not separated!" (D&C 135:3).

The Palmyra area was filled with religious excitement.

A VISION FROM GOD

Physical labor was not their entire focus. As Joseph wrote later: "There was in the place where we lived an unusual excitement on the subject of religion. . . . Great multitudes united themselves to the different religious parties, which created no small stir and division amongst the people. . . .

"I often said to myself: What is to be done? Who of all these parties are right; . . . and how shall I know it? . . .

"I was one day reading the Epistle of James, first chapter and fifth verse, which reads: *If any of you lack wisdom, let him ask of God, that giveth to all men liberally, and upbraideth not; and it shall be given him.*

"Never did any passage of scripture come with more power to the heart of man than this did at this time to mine. It seemed to enter with great force into every feeling of my heart. I reflected on it again and again, knowing that if any person needed wisdom from God, I did."

"At length I came to the conclusion that I must either remain in darkness and confusion, or else I must do as James directs, that is, ask of God. . . .

"I retired to the woods to make the attempt. It was on the morning of a beautiful, clear day, early in the spring of eighteen hundred and twenty. . . . I kneeled down and began to offer up the desires of my heart to God. . . . Immediately I was seized upon by some power which entirely overcame me. . . .

"Just at this moment of great alarm, I saw a pillar of light exactly over my head, above the brightness of the sun, which descended gradually until it fell upon me. . . .

"When the light rested upon me I saw two Personages, whose brightness and glory defy all description, standing above me in the air. One of them spake unto me, calling me by name and said, pointing to the other—*This is My Beloved Son. Hear Him!* . . .

"I asked the Personages who stood above me in the light, which of all the sects was right . . . and which I should join.

"I was answered that I must join none of them, for they were all wrong. . . .

"I saw a pillar of light exactly over my head, above the brightness of the sun, which descended gradually until it fell upon me."

"When the light had departed, I had no strength; but soon recovering in some degree, I went home."

The religions of that day taught that God was a Spirit in the sky, nowhere yet everywhere present. The true nature of our Heavenly Father had become perverted.

When young Joseph came out of the grove he had actually seen the Father and the Son. Joseph learned that man was truly made in the image of God, that God has a voice, that he is kind, and that he answers prayers. The Son is like the Father, yet a separate and distinct individual who is obedient to the Father in all things.

ears later, Joseph F. Smith, Hyrum's son, said this of his Uncle Joseph: "I love to contemplate the innocence and the artless simplicity of his boyhood. . . . How could a child at his age be impelled by other than honest motives? . . . He was much like other children; his play was like that of his companions; his thoughts, like those of most children, were innocent. . . . Though poor, his parents were honest and good; they delighted in the truth, and it was their honest desire to live according to the best light within them. Love and good will to all found expression in their hearts and actions, and their children were imbued with like sentiments."

Soon thereafter, Joseph told a minister about his experience. Joseph said, "He treated my communication not only lightly, but with great contempt, saying . . . that there were no such things as visions or revelations in these days."

Soon, like the wings of the wind, falsehoods, rumors, and slander flew in every direction. Joseph became the object of ridicule and persecution from all areas of society.

Joseph wondered why men of "high standing would take notice sufficient to excite the public mind against me, and create a bitter persecution." He was only "an obscure boy," but "all the sects" were "united to persecute me." He said, "It was often the cause of great sorrow to myself."

But, he said, "It was nevertheless a fact that I had beheld a vision. . . . I had actually seen a light, and in the midst of that light I saw two Personages, and they did in reality speak to me. . . . I knew it, and I knew that God knew it, and I could not deny it, neither dared I do it."

After Joseph told of his marvelous vision, he was subjected to whispering, lies, and ridicule.

A Growing Young Man

Joseph had received a vision that had changed his life forever—and would change the world. But still he lived in a world of work, and he had to do his part. He wrote:

"As my father's worldly circumstances were very limited, we were under the necessity of laboring with our hands, hiring out by day's work and otherwise, as we could get opportunity."

One woman later recalled how her father loved young Joseph Smith and often hired him to work with his boys. At the time she was about six years old. She remembered playing in the field one afternoon while Joseph and her brothers worked in the cornrows. When evening came she was too tired to walk home. Crying, she asked her brothers to carry her, but they refused. Joseph lifted her to his shoulders and carried her to their home.

At one point their minister criticized her father for hiring Joseph Smith. The minister had heard the story of Joseph's vision and thought he might be a bad influence on others.

He said that Joseph was the best worker he'd ever found.

The girl's father disagreed. He said that Joseph was the best worker he'd ever found. He said that when the boys of the neighborhood worked by themselves, they'd waste a lot of time arguing, quarreling, and fist-fighting. But when Joseph Smith worked with them the work went steadily forward, and he got the full worth of the wages he paid.

Joseph wrote of the early years after the First Vision: "I was . . . mingling with all kinds of society, . . . display[ing] the weakness of youth, and the foibles of human nature. . . . In making this confession, no one need suppose me guilty of any great or malignant sins. . . . But I was guilty of levity, and sometimes associated with jovial company. . . . But this will not seem very strange to any one who recollects my youth, and is acquainted with my native cheery temperament."

The angel Moroni appeared to Joseph in his bedroom.

Moroni and the Golden Plates

Because he had made mistakes, and because he hadn't received additional instructions from God, Joseph felt a desire to be forgiven of his sins. One night in his bedroom, he began to pray for that forgiveness. He also prayed that God would help him to know what he should do next.

"While I was thus in the act of calling upon God, I discovered a light appearing in my room, which continued to increase until the room was lighter than at noonday, when immediately a personage appeared at my bedside, standing in the air, for his feet did not touch the floor. . . .

"His whole person was glorious beyond description, and his countenance truly like lightning. . . . When I first looked upon him, I was afraid; but the fear soon left me.

"He called me by name, and said unto me that he was a messenger sent from the presence of God to me, and that his name was Moroni; that God had a work for me to do; and that my name should be had for good and evil among all . . . people."

Moroni told Joseph about a book that had been written on gold plates. The book gave a history of a people who had once lived on the American continent. The Lord wanted Joseph to get the plates and translate its message into English.

After the angel left, Joseph lay in his bed "marveling greatly." Suddenly he "discovered that [his] room was again beginning to get lighted, and in an instant, as it were, the same heavenly messenger was again by [his] bedside."

He related to Joseph the very same things as before and then told him of great judgments that were coming upon the earth. Then he left, as he had done before. After a short time the angel appeared for a third time with the same message as before. He also added a caution that Satan would tempt him to use the plates to get rich.

By then it was nearly time to get up. Joseph arose and went to work, but he was so exhausted that he didn't have the strength. His father could tell that Joseph wasn't feeling well and told him to go home. Joseph started to do so, but on the way he fainted from weakness.

"The first thing that I can recollect was a voice speaking unto me, calling me by name. I looked up, and beheld the same messenger standing over my head, surrounded by light as before." The angel repeated the instructions from the previous night, and then told Joseph to go tell his father.

"I obeyed; I returned to my father in the field, and rehearsed the whole matter to him. He replied to me that it was of God, and told me to go and do as commanded by the messenger."

The Smith family gathered together each evening to hear Joseph share the things he was learning.

In 1826, Joseph went to work for a man named Josiah Stoal. Since Stoal lived some distance from Joseph's home, he was given food and lodging at the home of a Mr. Isaac Hale, of Harmony, Pennsylvania. Joseph wrote: "It was there I first saw my wife, . . . Emma Hale [Isaac's daughter]. On the 18th of January, 1827, we were married." Joseph took Emma back to his father's home in New York and farmed with him that season.

Joseph said, "I left the field, and went to the place where the messenger had told me the plates were deposited."

Joseph found the place near the top of the largest hill in the area, about three miles from his home. There he saw a large stone that Moroni had shown him in vision. He found a lever and moved the stone. "I looked in, and there indeed did I behold the plates, . . . as stated by the messenger."

Joseph later reported, "I made an attempt to take them out, but was forbidden by the messenger." The angel told him that it would be four years before it would be time for Joseph to have the plates. In the meantime, Joseph was to meet the angel every year on that hillside for further preparations.

His mother, Lucy, wrote, "From this time forth Joseph continued to receive instructions, . . . and every evening we gathered our children together and gave our time up to the discussion of those things which he instructed to us."

And brother William added: "We all had the most implicit confidence in what he said. He was a truthful boy. Father and Mother believed him, why should not the children? . . . No, we never doubted his word for one minute."

Two months after the angel's visit to young Joseph, the Smith family suffered a great tragedy. Alvin developed an acute bowel disorder and within a few short days lay on his deathbed. As he said farewells to his brothers, sisters, and parents, Alvin told Joseph to "be a good boy and do whatever the angel tells you to do so you can get the records." The family mourned deeply.

Early in the morning of September 22, 1827, Joseph went to where the plates were buried and there received them from the angel Moroni. He also received the Urim and Thummim, which would help him translate the plates. Joseph then went to another location and hid the plates in a hollow log. He covered the hole in the log with bark.

A day or so later, Joseph went to a neighboring town to work for a widow. Joseph was still gone when his father overheard some people in Palmyra scheming to find the "golden Bible." Alarmed, Father Smith told Emma. She agreed to ride on a horse to where Joseph was working so she could warn him.

Joseph kept the spectacles-like Urim and Thummim with him. By looking into it he could tell if the ancient record was safe. While he was working for the widow, he looked into the Urim and Thummim and knew that Emma was coming. He walked down the road to meet her. She expressed her fears and told of the plot. Joseph calmed her by saying that he knew everything was all right—but he felt he should go move the plates. Excusing himself from the widow for a short period and borrowing a horse, he and Emma rushed back to the Smith farm.

In the thick woods about three miles from his home, Joseph approached the old birch log and found everything undisturbed. He took off a linen smock he had been wearing and wrapped the plates in it. Even though Joseph was a large and strong young man used to grueling physical labor, the approximately sixty-pound weight was very burdensome, and he decided to take a shortcut through the woods.

As Joseph was jumping over a tree in his path, a man attacked him from behind and hit Joseph with his gun. Staggering from the blow, Joseph turned and knocked the man down. Joseph then ran faster. Soon he was attacked again. Knocking the second man down, he ran on. A third time a man jumped out and struck him with a gun. In this final struggle, Joseph dislocated his thumb. Gasping for breath, he finally reached the safety of the house.

When Joseph received the plates, he had to run from three assailants as they attacked him, trying to get the plates.

After receiving the plates, Joseph examined them with great interest.

THE LOST PAGES

Unceasing persecution and efforts by others to get the records caused Joseph and Emma to move to her father's home in Pennsylvania, more than one hundred miles away. A prosperous farmer named Martin Harris gave Joseph fifty dollars to help them move.

After they settled in a small house near Emma's family, Martin Harris made the long trip to see how the work was progressing. Martin spent several weeks with the Smiths and acted as Joseph's scribe while he began translation of the plates. They completed 116 pages.

As Martin was preparing to go back home, he pleaded with Joseph to let him take the manuscript and show it to his skeptical wife and neighbors. Joseph prayed about the request, and the Lord said no. Joseph wanted to please Martin because Martin had been so helpful. Joseph was also desirous of finding more supporters—he had been persecuted and disbelieved for so long, he felt other believers would be a blessing. Joseph asked the Lord again, but the answer was no. Then Joseph asked a third time. Finally the Lord gave permission. But Martin had to follow strict restrictions about who he could show the pages to.

The day after Martin left, Emma gave birth to a baby boy. Joseph, along with Emma's mother and a midwife, attended to her needs. By the day's end, the baby had died and Emma herself was hovering near death.

When Joseph finally had a chance to examine the plates, he saw that "each plate was six inches wide, and eight inches long, and not quite so thick as common tin. They were filled with engravings, in Egyptian characters, and bound together in a volume as the leaves of a book, with three rings running through the whole. The volume was something near six inches in thickness, a part of which was sealed."

Martin Harris

After giving birth, Emma became very ill, nearly dying. Joseph attentively watched by her bedside.

With constant care Emma slowly began to recover. After three weeks she was still quite ill, but the fact that they had not heard from Martin weighed heavily on their minds. She finally encouraged Joseph to go back to the Palmyra area to see about the pages.

Joseph neither ate nor slept on that doleful journey. He was fearful that he had offended God in pressing for Martin to take the translation, concerned "that he had regarded man more than his Maker."

Joseph was waiting at his parents' home when Martin finally came to the door. Martin sat down with a glum and morose look. Hyrum asked Martin if he was sick. Lucy recorded what happened next:

"Martin pressed his hands upon his temples and cried out in a tone of anguish, 'Oh! I have lost my soul. I have lost my soul.'

"Oh, my God, my God. . . . All is lost, is lost!"

Sick with worry, Joseph waited for Martin to return with the manuscript pages.

"Joseph, who had smothered his fears till now, sprang from the table, exclaiming, 'Oh Martin, have you lost that manuscript? Have you broken your oath and brought down condemnation upon my head as well as your own?'

"'Yes,' replied Martin, 'It is gone and I know not where.'

"'Oh, my God, my God,' said Joseph. . . . 'All is lost, is lost! What shall I do? I have sinned. . . .' And he wept and groaned, walking the floor continually. . . . I besought him not to mourn so. . . . But what could I say to comfort him . . . ? The next morning he went home. We parted with heavy hearts."

The entire family mourned. As far as they knew, all was indeed lost!

As a consequence of Joseph's choices, Moroni took the plates so Joseph could not continue the translation. But after a season of prayer and repentance, Joseph again received the plates and was able to continue the translation.

THE LORD SENDS
ANOTHER SCRIBE

With Martin Harris gone, Joseph needed another scribe to help him in the translation process. In April 1829, Oliver Cowdery arrived. He had met the Smith family in Palmyra, and they had told him about the plates. Oliver had then traveled to Harmony, Pennsylvania, to meet Joseph and to learn what he could about his story.

He felt the truthfulness of Joseph's testimony; and two days after he arrived, he began to help Joseph with the translation.

From April to July the two young men diligently worked on the translation. They labored long hours, taking only short breaks to rest and to eat the meals that Emma prepared.

Oliver Cowdery described these events by writing: "These were days never to be forgotten—to sit under the sound of a voice dictated by the inspiration of heaven, awakened the utmost gratitude of this bosom! Day after day I continued, uninterrupted, to write from his mouth, as he translated with the Urim and Thummim . . . the history or record called 'The Book of Mormon.'"

Oliver Cowdery assisted Joseph in the translation of the Book of Mormon.

Joseph Smith and Oliver Cowdery received the Aaronic Priesthood from John the Baptist.

THE RESTORATION OF THE PRIESTHOOD

As Joseph and Oliver worked on the translation of the Book of Mormon, they came across passages about the necessity of baptism and other ordinances. Since they knew they had no authority for such ordinances, they wondered what to do.

Joseph recorded: "We . . . went into the woods to pray and inquire of the Lord respecting baptism for the remission of sins, that we found mentioned in the translation of the plates. While we were thus employed, praying and calling upon the Lord, a messenger from heaven descended in a cloud of light, and having laid his hands upon us, he ordained us, saying:

"*Upon you my fellow servants, in the name of Messiah, I confer the Priesthood of Aaron, which holds the keys of the ministering of angels, and of the gospel of repentance, and of baptism by immersion for the remission of sins. . . .*

"He commanded us to go and be baptized, and gave us directions. . . .

"Accordingly we went and were baptized. I baptized him [Oliver] first, and afterwards he baptized me. . . .

"The messenger who visited . . . said that his name was John, the same that is called John the Baptist in the New Testament, and that he acted under the direction of Peter, James and John, who held the keys of the Priesthood of Melchizedek, which Priesthood, he said, would in due time be conferred on us. . . . We were filled with the Holy Ghost, and rejoiced in the God of our salvation."

After receiving the Aaronic Priesthood, Joseph Smith baptized Oliver Cowdery.

THE THREE WITNESSES

The angel Moroni gave Joseph strict instructions not to show the gold plates to anyone unless the Lord commanded it. In June 1829, Martin Harris, David Whitmer, and Oliver Cowdery learned that the Lord was going to designate three witnesses who would see the ancient record. They asked Joseph if they might have that privilege. Joseph inquired of the Lord, who said they could.

An angel showed the plates to Oliver Cowdery and David Whitmer.

With Joseph, the three men went to a wooded area near the Whitmer home. They began to pray with much faith to Almighty God. Starting with Joseph, each man prayed fervently to obtain some divine manifestation. Nothing happened. They each prayed again. Still nothing happened.

Martin Harris, feeling his sins were preventing the revelation, withdrew from the group. The remaining three knelt down again and shortly an exceedingly bright light appeared above them, and then an angel stood before them holding the plates in his hands. He turned over the leaves one by one, so they could see them and the engravings.

Joseph Smith said: "We heard a voice from out of the bright light above us, saying: 'These plates have been revealed by the power of God, and they have been translated by the power of God. The translation of them which you have seen is correct, and I command you to bear record of what you now see and hear.'"

Joseph then joined Martin Harris, and Martin also received a vision.

Lucy Mack Smith wrote: "When Joseph came in, he threw himself down beside me: 'Father! Mother!' said he. 'You do not know how happy I am. The Lord has caused the plates to be shown to three more besides me, who have also seen an angel and will have to testify to the truth of what I have said. For they know for themselves that I do not go about to deceive the people.'"

When the translation was completed, Joseph Smith delivered the manuscript to a printer in Palmyra, E. B. Grandin. Grandin started the typesetting in August 1829 and finished printing the book in March 1830.

Joseph wrote: "The Book of Mormon . . . had now been published . . . and as the ancient prophet had predicted of it, 'it was accounted as a strange thing.' No small stir was created by its appearance. Great opposition and much persecution followed the believers of its authenticity. But it had now come to pass that truth had sprung out of the earth, and righteousness had looked down from heaven, so we feared not our opponents, knowing that we had both truth and righteousness on our side."

We declare with words of soberness, that an angel of God came down from heaven, and . . . that we beheld and saw the plates."
—THE THREE WITNESSES

Joseph Smith received the first copy of the Book of Mormon in March 1830.

Family, friends, and other supporters traveled to the Whitmer home for the organization of the Church.

THE BEGINNINGS OF THE CHURCH

Around noon on April 6, 1830, about fifty people gathered at the log cabin home of Peter Whitmer to witness the most significant thing in their lives: the organization of the restored Church of Jesus Christ. The small home was filled to overflowing.

The twenty-four-year-old Prophet Joseph Smith, having been authorized and directed by God, conducted the business of the meeting.

He later wrote: "The Holy Ghost was poured out upon us to a very great degree—some prophesied, whilst we all praised the Lord, and rejoiced exceedingly. . . . Several persons . . . came forward . . . and were received into the Church; . . . my own father and mother were baptized, to my great joy and consolation; and about the same time, Martin Harris and Orrin Porter Rockwell."

> **P**raise to my God! I have lived to see my own father baptized into the true Church of Jesus Christ!' [Joseph] wept aloud for joy as did Joseph of old when he beheld his father coming up into the land of Egypt."
>
> —LUCY MACK SMITH

Joseph Smith conducted the meeting when the Church was organized on April 6, 1830.

Missionaries traveled to the frontiers of Missouri to take the Book of Mormon to the Native Americans.

Shortly after the Book of Mormon was published, the Lord called several missionaries to take its message to the Native Americans, including those on the Missouri frontier.

On their way, the missionaries preached in Kirtland, Ohio. Their message caused considerable excitement, and a branch of the Church began to grow there.

Parley P. Pratt wrote of the journey to Missouri: "We travelled on foot for . . . hundred[s of] miles through vast prairies . . . no beaten road; houses few and far between. . . . We travelled for whole days, from morning till night, without a house or fire, wading in snow to the knees at every step, and the cold so intense . . . even in the mid-day sun, for nearly six weeks. We carried on our backs our changes of clothing, several books, and corn bread and raw pork. We often ate our frozen bread and pork by the way, when the bread would be so frozen that we could not bite or penetrate any part of it but the outside crust.

"After much fatigue and some suffering we all arrived in Independence, in the county of Jackson, on the extreme western frontiers of Missouri, and of the United States."

Meanwhile, persecution in New York had become so

Because of persecution and bogus arrests in
New York, Joseph Smith and the Saints
were commanded to move to Ohio.

intense that wherever Joseph went to teach he was hounded with bogus arrests and threatened with violence. Finally, the Lord commanded him and the Saints to "go to the Ohio" (D&C 37:1; see also D&C 38:32).

Joseph and Emma borrowed a sleigh from Joseph Knight and traveled to Kirtland, accompanied by two new converts from Ohio, Sydney Rigdon and Edward Partridge. Emma was seven months pregnant and expecting twins.

Among the people whom the missionaries met in the Kirtland, Ohio, area were Newel and Elizabeth Ann Whitney. Elizabeth related an experience that occurred shortly before

they met the missionaries: "One night—it was midnight—as my husband and I, in our house at Kirtland, were praying to the Father to be shown the way, the spirit rested upon us and a cloud overshadowed the house. . . . Then we heard a voice out of the cloud saying: 'Prepare to receive the word of the Lord, for it is coming!' At this we marveled greatly; but from that moment we knew that the word of the Lord was coming to Kirtland."

While yet in New York, Joseph had seen Newel and Elizabeth Whitney in a vision, kneeling in prayer, asking the Lord to send the prophet to Kirtland.

Joseph first met Newel K. Whitney in the Gilbert and Whitney store.

On arriving in Kirtland, Joseph jumped out of the sleigh he and Emma were riding in and went into the Gilbert and Whitney store, where he exclaimed to the proprietor, "Newel K. Whitney! Thou art the man!"

Brother Whitney was bewildered and responded with, "I could not call you by name as you have me."

Then came the reply, "I am Joseph the Prophet. You have prayed me here, now what do you want of me?"

Not long after, Joseph and Emma settled in Hiram, about thirty miles southeast of Kirtland. There they lived in the home of John and Alice Johnson. It was a secluded and peaceful place. Many conferences and meetings were held in the home.

That summer, the Prophet and other leading elders were commanded by the Lord to make a trip to Missouri. When he arrived, the missionaries there greeted him with rejoicing and tears. The brethren then gave Joseph a tour of the surrounding area. As he observed this new land, he praised God for the bounty contained in the beautiful rolling prairies, the soil rich and fertile, as well as a climate that seemed ideal.

While he was in Missouri, the Lord said to him: "This land, which is the land of Missouri, . . . is the land which I have appointed and consecrated for the gathering of the saints. Wherefore, this is the land of promise, and the place for the city of Zion" (D&C 57:1–2).

Hundreds of faithful members soon made their way to Missouri, hoping to build a temple and establish a community of faithful followers of the Lord Jesus Christ.

While Joseph was in Missouri, he surveyed the beauty of the countryside.

A SEASON OF GROWTH AND JOY

The Saints in Missouri had to build their community from the ground up. Western Missouri was on the outskirts of the American frontier. Missouri had been a state for only ten years, and Independence—where the Saints were settling—was only four years old. As frontiers tend to be, it was wild and woolly.

Missouri had few white settlers. All of Jackson County had only a little over 2,800 people in the 1830 census. By the summer of 1832, however, over 900 Saints had gathered at Independence, some of them new converts from Great Britain.

The Saints built their Missouri homes from scratch.

Jackson County, Missouri, was on the outskirts of the American frontier.

A Work to Fill the Earth

At one point Joseph Smith gathered with a small group of members in Kirtland. Wilford Woodruff recorded a prophecy Joseph made in the meeting: "On Sunday night the Prophet called on all who held the Priesthood to gather into the little log school house they had there. It was a small house, perhaps 14 feet square. But it held the whole of the Priesthood of the Church of Jesus Christ of Latter-day Saints who were then in the town of Kirtland. . . . When they got through [bearing testimonies] the Prophet said, 'Brethren I have been very much edified and instructed in your testimonies here tonight, but I want to say to you before the Lord, that you know no more concerning the destinies of this Church and kingdom than a babe upon its mother's lap. You don't comprehend it.' I was rather surprised. He said, 'It is only a little handful of Priesthood you see here tonight, but this Church will fill North and South America—it will fill the world."

At the same time some of the Saints were moving to Missouri, others were building up Kirtland. And as the Church began to be established in Kirtland, the Lord commanded the Saints to build a temple.

To many, this seemed to be an impossible requirement. The area around Kirtland was having economic problems—as was the entire nation. Many Church members were poor and in great need. And persecution continued.

Under those circumstances, how could they build a temple?

Joseph raised the question in a meeting of the Brethren. He asked each one to stand and express his feelings. Some thought it would be better to build a frame house. Others argued that a frame house would be too costly. Most felt a log house would be best.

Then Joseph stood. "And shall we, brethren, build a house for our God [with] logs? No, I have a better plan than that. I have a plan of the house of the Lord, given by himself."

Joseph then led the brethren outside and said, "Now brethren, let us go select a place for the building." He led them to a field of wheat, which he and his brothers had sown the previous autumn, and selected a spot in the northwest corner. Hyrum ran to the house and grabbed a scythe. "We are preparing to build a house for the Lord," he said to his mother, "and I am determined to be the first at the work."

For a time, despite occasional storms, Kirtland was a haven for the Saints.

The Lord's work in Kirtland was proceeding in other ways as well. Joseph organized the School of the Prophets and taught the gospel in many settings. The Lord revealed the Word of Wisdom at one of these meetings, teaching the Saints some rules of good health. For instance, they were to avoid tobacco and alcohol as well as hot drinks such as coffee and tea. Upon receiving this instruction, the Brethren threw their pipes, tobacco, and chew plugs into the fireplace.

In Missouri, the Saints were instructed to set up a printing establishment. There they printed a periodical called *The Evening and Morning Star.* They also prepared to print the Book of Commandments, which contained many of the revelations the Lord had given to Joseph Smith.

The Saints were baptized wherever there was enough water—including in icy streams, when necessary.

By the summer of 1833 the membership of the Church in Jackson County, Missouri, numbered more than one thousand souls. Parley P. Pratt wrote, "These had all purchased lands and paid for them, and most of them were improving in buildings and in cultivation. Peace and plenty had crowned their labors, and the wilderness became a fruitful field, and the solitary place began to bud and blossom as the rose. . . . There has seldom, if ever, been a happier people upon the earth than the Church of the Saints now were."

"There has seldom, if ever, been a happier people upon the earth than the Church of the Saints now were."

Mormon families built up the Missouri frontier in a spirit of faith and hope.

As missionaries went forth to different parts of the United States and Canada, many converts joined the Church. The mother of Margaret Pierce had an experience that was not atypical. Margaret wrote later: "Word came that the Prophet Joseph Smith was to visit our Branch. . . . So animated with loving kindness, so mild and gentle, yet big and powerful and majestic was the Prophet, that to me he seemed more than a man; I thought almost, that he was an angel. We were all investigating, none of my people had yet entered the waters

of baptism. It was 2 o'clock in the morning before we permitted him to retire. We wanted to listen to him all night. . . .

"The very next day my mother was ready for baptism. The ice was six inches deep, but was cut, and the way was prepared, and Mother entered the waters of baptism. She was baptized by Elder Lorenzo Barnes, and was confirmed a member of the Church of Jesus Christ of Latter-day Saints by the Prophet Joseph Smith."

The Church was moving forward in another magnificent and very important way. The Kirtland Temple, begun in 1833, was completed in the spring of 1836. The Lord revealed a marvelous dedicatory prayer, which the Prophet offered on March 27, 1836.

Joseph prayed "that Thy glory may rest down upon thy people, and upon this thy house, which we now dedicate to thee, that it may be sanctified and consecrated to be holy, and that thy holy presence may be continually in this house; and that all people who shall enter upon the threshold of the Lord's house may feel thy power, and feel constrained to acknowledge that thou hast sanctified it, and that it is thy house, a place of thy holiness." (D&C 109:12–13.)

The dedication was accompanied by marvelous heavenly manifestations: "A noise was heard like the sound of a rushing

" A noise was heard like the sound of a rushing mighty wind, . . . and I beheld the Temple was filled with angels."

mighty wind, which filled the Temple, and all the congregation simultaneously arose, being moved upon by an invisible power; many began to speak in tongues and prophesy; others saw glorious visions; and I beheld the Temple was filled with angels, which fact I declared to the congregation. The people of the neighborhood came running together (hearing an unusual sound within, and seeing a bright light like a pillar of fire resting upon the Temple), and were astonished at what was taking place."

One week after the dedication, Joseph Smith and Oliver Cowdery experienced marvelous manifestations in the temple. The resurrected Jesus Christ came in glory to accept the temple. Moses, Elias, and Elijah returned with keys of the priesthood. "The hearts of thousands and tens of thousands shall greatly rejoice in consequence of the blessings which shall be poured out . . . in this house," the Savior said. (D&C 110:9.)

The dedication of the Kirtland Temple in 1836 was accompanied by marvelous heavenly manifestations.

When Wilford Woodruff first met Joseph, the Prophet was "shooting at a mark."

Throughout Joseph's life there was much curiosity about this man who was called a prophet. There are almost as many different stories of first meetings with the Prophet as there are people who met him.

Wilford Woodruff first met the Prophet in Kirtland, April 25, 1834. He found Joseph and Hyrum having target practice with a brace of pistols. "Brother Woodruff," Joseph said while shaking his hand heartily, "I've been out shooting at a mark, and I wanted to see if I could hit anything." Wilford replied, "There is no law against a man shooting at a mark, that I know of."

Joseph then indicated a nearby wolf skin he wanted for a wagon seat and asked if Wilford would help him tan it. "I pulled off my coat," wrote Wilford Woodruff, "stretched the skin across the back of a chair, and soon had it tanned—although I had to smile at my first experience with the Prophet."

Joseph recorded: "This morning, a minister from Connecticut, by the name of John W. Olived, called at my house. . . . The first question he asked me, after passing a compliment was: 'How many members have you in your Church?' I replied that we had between fifteen hundred and two thousand in this branch. He then asked: 'Wherein do you differ from other Christian denominations?' I replied, that we believe the Bible, and they do not. However, he affirmed that he believed the Bible. . . . But when I laid before him the principles of the Gospel, viz: faith and repentance; baptism, for the remission of sins; and the laying on of hands, for the reception of the Holy Ghost, he manifested much surprise. . . . The man appeared astonished at our doctrine, but by no means hostile."

Mobbers from Missouri ordered Mormons to leave or be killed.

PERSECUTIONS INCREASE

Even though the Church prospered, its enemies continued to be active.

For example, on the night of March 24, 1832, a mob with blackened faces dragged Joseph from his home into a nearby field. There he was beaten, tarred and feathered, and nearly killed. Sidney Rigdon, Joseph's counselor, received the same horrific treatment.

The Saints in Missouri were likewise afflicted. On July 20, 1833, a mob of 300 to 400 men gathered at Independence. They destroyed the printing office (which was a two-story brick building). They stripped the clothes off Edward Partridge, the first bishop of the Church, then tarred and feathered and beat him. They "threatened death and destruction to all the saints if they did not leave the country."

Some of the faithful brethren were stripped, tarred, and feathered by the mobs.

The mobs destroyed homes and forced people to flee without food or belongings.

In the night, the Saints saw a marvelous display of falling stars.

On other occasions, mobs attacked members of the Church, destroying their homes and threatening to kill the Saints if they did not leave the area. After the Saints were forced out of Jackson County in late 1833, Parley P. Pratt wrote:

"While we thus made our escape companies of ruffians were ranging the county . . . bursting into houses . . . frightening women and children, and threatening to kill them if they did not flee immediately. . . . The shore began to be lined on both sides of the ferry with men, women and children. . . . The ferry was constantly employed.

"Some families were fortunate to escape together with some provisions, while hundreds of people were trying to flee from the armed and roving mobs leaving homes, provisions, household goods, livestock and properties of all kinds behind. Some were in tents and others in the open rain as it descended in torrents. Husbands, wives and children who had become separated were trying to find one another."

The next night was clear. While the Saints stayed in tents or under the stars, Parley P. Pratt wrote, their hearts were cheered by a sign sent from above:

"About two o'clock [in the] morning we were called up by the cry of signs in the heavens. We arose, and to our great astonishment all the firmament seemed enveloped in splendid fireworks, as if every star in the broad expanse had been hurled from its course, and sent lawless through the wilds of . . . space in every direction, with long trains of light following in their course. This lasted for several hours. . . . Every heart was filled with joy at this majestic display of signs and wonders, showing the near approach of the coming of the Son of God."

The men of Zion's Camp traveled nearly a thousand miles as they made their way to Missouri.

When word of the Missouri depredations reached Kirtland, Joseph Smith and the other Saints were greatly concerned about the Church in Missouri. As the Prophet pondered the problem, the Lord gave him a revelation telling him to gather a band of righteous men to go to the rescue of the Saints in Missouri (see D&C 103). This group was called Zion's Camp.

In sending them forth, the Lord said, "All victory and glory is brought to pass unto you through your diligence, faithfulness, and prayers of faith." (D&C 103:36.)

Zion's Camp included 204 men, led by Joseph Smith. They left Kirtland in May 1834, and reached Clay County, Missouri, almost two months later. The long and difficult journey covered nearly a thousand miles—one way.

In the end, the Lord told Joseph that he would not require the men to fight but that He would redeem Zion in other ways.

Joseph Bates Noble recorded his experience with Zion's Camp by saying, "In the Spring of 1834 I settled up my business because there was a proclamation made by the servants of God that the strength of his house was needed to go to Missouri to redeem Zion. . . . I accordingly volunteered, bid farewell to my father's family and all my acquaintances. . . .

"We organized ourselves into companies of tens and fifties and hundreds. . . . We received much good instruction from President Joseph Smith from time to time as circumstances would permit. . . .

"We organized ourselves into companies of tens and fifties and hundreds. . . . We received much good instruction from President Joseph Smith."

"The Lord blessed us in a wonderful manner. We could see and feel that his care was over us. By his might and power we were preserved. Many were taken sick on the way. They were administered to and soon well. . . . President Joseph Smith received the word of the Lord, saying our offering was accepted, comparative to that of Abraham. Our hearts rejoiced when they heard this."

While the Church was experiencing persecution from without, it also had great enemies attacking from within. Many in Kirtland began to doubt their testimonies, and in 1837 huge numbers left the Church, proclaiming that Joseph Smith was a fallen prophet.

Joseph was undeterred. He continued to seek the will of the Lord for his own life and for the Church, doing what was required regardless of the sacrifice.

At the height of the Kirtland apostasy, the Lord commanded Joseph to send missionaries to England.

Heber C. Kimball recorded: "On Sunday, the 4th day of June, 1837, the Prophet Joseph came to me, . . . and whispering to me, said, 'Brother Heber, the Spirit of the Lord has whispered to me: Let my servant Heber go to England and proclaim my Gospel, and open the door of salvation to that nation.'"

The first time I saw Joseph Smith was at Far West, in 1837. There were but three houses in town at that time. On the south side of the elder Peter Whitmer's house was a wagon with a box on. Here were seated Joseph, Sidney Rigdon and others. . . . Said he, '. . . The Book of Mormon is true, just what it purports to be, and for this testimony I expect to give an account in the day of judgment. . . . If I obtain the glory which I have in view I expect to wade through much tribulation.'

"In closing his remarks he said, 'The Savior declared the time was coming when secret or hidden things should be revealed on the house tops. Well,' says he, 'I have revealed to you a few things, if not on the house top, on the wagon top.'

"On another occasion he preached and chastised the rich, or those who had money, for buying land at government price and selling it in small lots to their poor brethren at a high price. He said the Lord was not pleased with their conduct. 'You say I am a Prophet. Well, then, I will prophesy, and when you go home write it down and remember it. You think you have been badly treated by your enemies; but if you don't do better than you are now doing, I prophesy that the state of Missouri will not hold you. Your sufferings have hardly commenced.'

"I think about eighteen months after this we all left the state."

—DAVID OSBORN

Joseph and some of his associates were captured by the Missouri militia.

Even though the Saints fled the mobs in one area of Missouri, persecution continued to follow them. A militia of five thousand men, including many enemies to the Church, marched to Far West in October 1838. Joseph Smith, who had moved from Kirtland to escape persecution there, went out to meet the leaders of the militia. Joseph carried a white flag of truce.

Instead of honoring the truce, the leader of the militia turned to the Church's enemies in the militia, "Gentlemen, I now deliver to you Joseph Smith, Jr., the Mormon prophet. He is now in your hands as your prisoner.

Joseph Holbrook recorded what happened next: "At this moment the lines of our enemies began to ring with the most hideous yells that the Saints ever heard and could be heard for some miles around, of their achieved and treacherous victory. It was with the greatest trouble that they could keep their enemies from shooting them down as wild beasts in their camp. There was a court martial held in which they condemned the prisoners [Joseph, Hyrum, and others] to be shot on the public square in Far West."

The Saints were driven out of their Missouri homes, ordered to leave under threat of death.

The planned execution was not carried out. The ranking officer, Brigadier General Alexander Doniphan, refused to carry out the order. Instead, Joseph Smith, Hyrum Smith, Sidney Rigdon, Parley P. Pratt, and others were placed in covered wagons and hauled sixty miles to Independence and then to Richmond. There they were held for trial.

While the Prophet was in jail, the Saints were being hounded from the state. The governor of Missouri, Lilburn Boggs, signed the order that "the Mormons must be treated as enemies and *must be exterminated* or driven from the state."

It seemed as if the hounds of hell had been let loose upon the Saints. Mormon women and children were driven from their homes with little or nothing in the middle of winter and threatened with their lives if they didn't leave immediately. Men were hunted down and imprisoned at the point of bayonet.

After Governor Boggs signed the extermination order, the Saints took what belongings they could and gradually moved to Illinois.

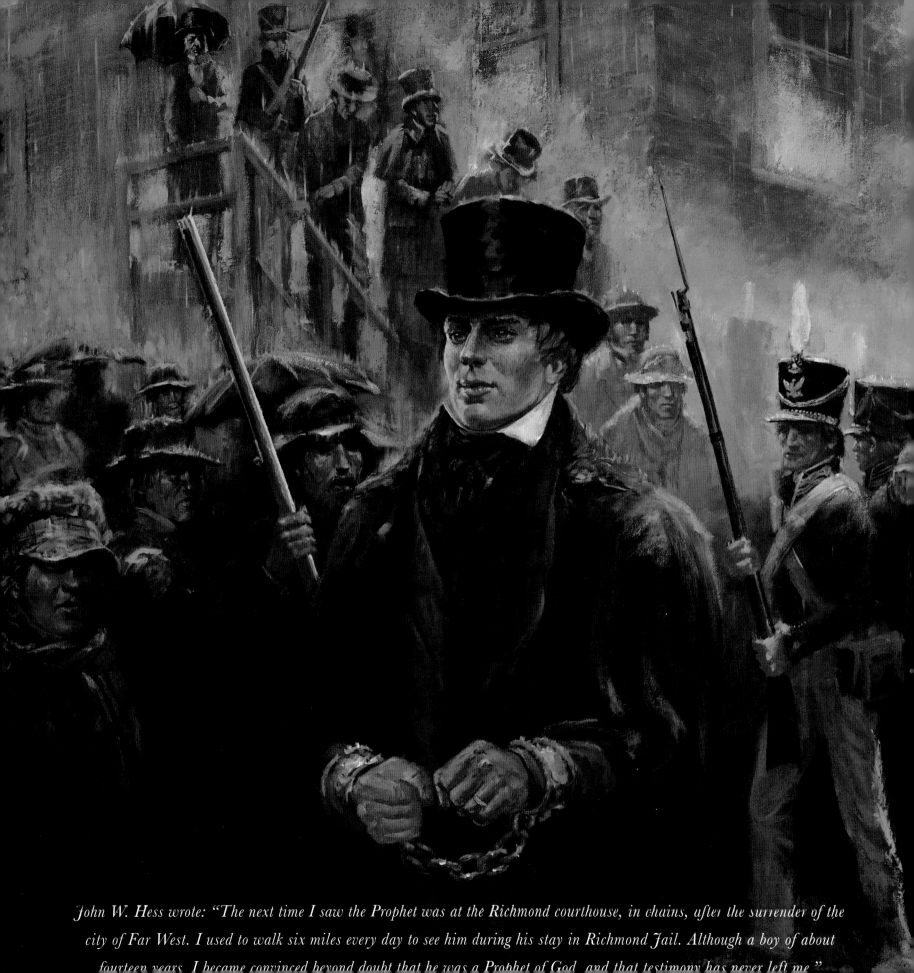

John W. Hess wrote: "The next time I saw the Prophet was at the Richmond courthouse, in chains, after the surrender of the city of Far West. I used to walk six miles every day to see him during his stay in Richmond Jail. Although a boy of about fourteen years, I became convinced beyond doubt that he was a Prophet of God, and that testimony has never left me."

Joseph and more than fifty other Latter-day Saint prisoners were kept in Richmond Jail for most of the month of November 1838, chained together in a building without a roof. At one point the guards were acting so coarse and profane that Joseph Smith stood and rebuked them—and they begged his forgiveness.

On the last day of November, Joseph and several others were transferred to a jail in nearby Liberty, Missouri. They were kept there for four-and-a-half months. The jail was drafty, cold, and crowded. The ceiling was so low that Joseph and his friends were unable to stand anytime during that period.

Discouraged and feeling helpless, Joseph cried out in prayer: "O God, where art thou? And where is the pavilion that covereth thy hiding place? How long shall thy hand be stayed, and thine eye, yea thy pure eye, behold from the eternal heavens the wrongs of thy people and of thy servants, and thine ear be penetrated with their cries? Yea, O Lord, how long shall they suffer these wrongs and unlawful oppressions?" (D&C 121:1–3).

In response to that prayer, the Lord gave reassuring words of comfort:

"My son, peace be unto thy soul; thine adversity and thine afflictions shall be but a small moment; and then, if thou endure it well, God shall exalt thee on high; thou shalt triumph over all thy foes. Thy friends do stand by thee, and they shall hail thee again with warm hearts and friendly hands" (D&C 121:7–9).

When Joseph and Hyrum Smith were taken to Independence in a covered wagon, guards prevented family and friends from going to the wagon to share expressions of love and comfort.

Joseph rejoiced in his days of peace with his family in Nauvoo, located on the banks of the Mississippi River.

During a time of great sickness, Joseph visited the afflicted, blessing them and healing many through the power of God.

PEACE IN NAUVOO

After Joseph had spent several months in Liberty Jail, he was transferred to Boone County. On the way a guard helped him to escape. Joseph made a long and treacherous journey across Missouri to Illinois, where he was reunited with his family.

Dimick Huntington was one of the first to see Joseph arrive. Dimick wrote: "I . . . saw Joseph land from the Quincy ferryboat about 8 o'clock in morning. He was dressed in an old pair of boots full of holes, pants torn, tucked inside of boots, blue cloak with collar turned up, wide brim black hat, rim sloped down, not been shaved for some time, looked pale and haggard. . . . When I got within about sixteen feet of him he raised his head. I exclaimed, My goodness, is it you, Brother Joseph? He raised his hand and stopped me saying, Hush, Hush. . . . Joseph not knowing the universal friendly feelings that existed in Quincy, was fearful he might be arrested again."

Only three days after arriving in Illinois, Joseph made a survey of the general area to locate a gathering place for the Saints. He settled on a place near Commerce, Illinois. He later named the new city Nauvoo.

The Saints, who had become homeless, were forced to live in tents on both sides of the Mississippi River. In July many of them became very ill. Joseph himself got sick and found it difficult to get out of bed. But he forced himself to get up and move among the people in their tents, giving them blessings. The Saints experienced a miraculous day of healing.

Lieutenant General Joseph Smith

One young lady wrote: "Some of the most impressive moments of my life were when I saw the Nauvoo Legion on parade with the Prophet (then General Joseph Smith) . . . on horseback at the head of the troops. It was indeed an imposing sight."

Joseph Smith was impressive in other ways. On one occasion he came upon a large group of young men who were wrestling. One of them was a bully who had thrown everyone he wrestled. Joseph agreed to join in the fun.

The bully was "eager to have a tussle with the Prophet," as one observer recorded. "The first pass he made Joseph whirled him around and took him by the collar and seat of his trousers and walked out to a ditch and threw him in it." Then Joseph took him by the arm and helped him back up. "You must not mind this," the Prophet said. "When I am with the boys I make all the fun I can for them."

The Mormons arrived in Nauvoo stripped of nearly everything, and the town scarcely existed. In the years that followed, they built a large and beautiful city. At one point it was probably the second largest city in Illinois.

Five years in Nauvoo gave the people a time of relative peace and prosperity, truly a gift from God.

Even in a time of peace, however, the Saints knew they needed protection. Accordingly, following the practice of the times, Joseph Smith formed the Nauvoo Legion. Every able-bodied man in Nauvoo was required to serve. Joseph Smith served as the lieutenant general of the legion.

Joseph Smith enjoyed wrestling and having fun with "the boys."

The Saints had not lived in Nauvoo for long before they began to build a new temple to the Lord. The Prophet personally worked on the temple, and he also often visited others working there.

Wandle Mace recorded that when Joseph "joined us on the temple grounds . . . we were sure of a rare treat. . . . Someone present . . . would say, 'Brother Joseph talk to us.'" He would say, 'What do you want me to talk about? Start something.' Soon a conversation would bring out some question for Joseph to answer, and then I could lean back and listen. Ah, what pleasure this gave me; he would unravel the scriptures and explain doctrine as no other man could. What had been mystery, he made so plain it was no longer mystery."

Joseph Smith directed details of the construction of the Nauvoo Temple.

Joseph enjoyed meeting the Saints when they arrived in Nauvoo.

Nauvoo is located on the banks of the Mississippi River. As missionaries went forth to other areas—and other nations—they brought back with them many converts. The city grew and swelled.

Joseph Smith often liked to greet people as they arrived in Nauvoo. Lucy Meserve Smith recalled her first meeting with the Prophet:

"I first met the Prophet Joseph Smith on a steamboat, when I landed at the ferry in Nauvoo. The first words he said to our company were: 'I guess you are all Latter-day Saints here, by the singing I heard when the boat landed.' He then shook hands with each one in the company, and then took his sister, Lucy [Smith] Millican's seven months' old boy in his

When Joseph and Emma lived in Nauvoo, they would occasionally ride out to their nearby farm.

arms and sat down and wept for joy, as his sister was thought to be in a decline when she left home the year before with her husband. She was indeed the picture of health when she returned, which gave the Prophet double joy on meeting her with her son."

On the rare times when he could find an opportunity,

Joseph liked to go out riding with Emma. She was an expert horsewoman. Joseph's journal entry for March 19, 1843, reads, "Rode out with Emma and visited my farm; returned about eleven, A.M., and spent the remainder of the day at home."

Joseph Smith wrote the Articles of Faith as part of the Wentworth letter in 1842.

> **J**oseph and some of the young men were playing various outdoor games, among which was a game of ball. By and by they began to get weary. He saw it, and calling them together he said: 'Let us build a log cabin.' So off they went, Joseph and the young men, to build a log cabin for a widow woman. Such was Joseph's way, always assisting in whatever he could."
>
> —EDWIN HOLDMAN

The years in Nauvoo were rich in an increase in doctrinal understanding. The Lord revealed much truth about temples, eternal marriage, and the role of women in the Church.

In early 1842, Joseph was asked by a newspaper editor in Chicago, John Wentworth, to explain what Mormons believe. Joseph responded by telling the history of his first vision, the Book of Mormon, and the establishment and persecutions of the Church. The Prophet also wrote the inspired Articles of Faith.

The Articles of Faith are a powerful explanation of many truths in the restored gospel.

"We believe in God, the Eternal Father, and in His Son, Jesus Christ, and in the Holy Ghost," the Prophet wrote. "We believe that through the Atonement of Christ, all mankind may be saved, by obedience to the laws and ordinances of the Gospel."

He mentioned the need for faith and repentance, for baptism and receiving the Holy Ghost. He spoke of the need for apostles and prophets. He listed some of the gifts of the Spirit and bore testimony of the Bible and Book of Mormon. He emphasized the need for continuing revelation and gave many other truths.

The Articles of Faith explained the basic truths in the gospel of Jesus Christ. They continue to be a blessing to many people, in many languages.

I have been present at meetings of the Relief Society and heard him give directions and counsel to the sisters, calculated to inspire them to efforts which would lead to celestial glory and exaltation, and oh! how my heart rejoiced!"

—MERCY THOMPSON

Joseph Smith organized the Relief Society of the Church in Nauvoo in March 1842. He said in one of their meetings, "The organization of the Church of Christ was never perfect until the women were organized."

On another occasion he said: "Our women have always been signalized for their acts of benevolence and kindness. . . . They will fly to the relief of the stranger; they will pour in oil and wine to the wounded heart of the distressed; they will dry up the tears of the orphan and make the widow's heart to rejoice."

The Lord directed Joseph to organize the women of the Church into the Relief Society.

People enjoyed Joseph's friendship, his wisdom, and his company. Emma wrote about Joseph's personal magnetism, "I never wanted him to go into the garden to work, for if he did, it would not be fifteen minutes before there would be three or four or sometimes a half dozen men 'round him and they would tramp the ground down faster than he could hoe it up."

Even though Nauvoo was flourishing, the specter of hate and antagonism was never far away. Joseph was constantly under the threat of violence, harassment, kidnapping, and arrest. Rumors and false stories incited people in neighboring communities and around the country to believe the worst about this new religion.

Joseph's greatest heartbreak was not from the enemies that surrounded him from Missouri or other parts of Illinois, but it was from those he thought were his friends in the Church, even among the leadership.

As the winter of 1844 turned into spring, the threat of war, destruction, and murder surrounded the Saints. Parley P. Pratt wrote to Joseph: "Dear Brother Joseph: . . . This is to forewarn you that you have a snake in the grass—a base traitor and hypocrite in your midst, of whom perhaps you may not be fully aware."

Unfortunately, there was more than one snake in the grass. Many of the Prophet's closest associates turned against him over the years—Thomas B. Marsh, William W. Phelps, Oliver Cowdery, William and Wilson Law, and many others. Some sought to defame him in the press. Others collaborated with legal authorities to haul him into court and to jail.

In 1843 and 1844, things got worse. A number of Joseph's former friends began to conspire to have him killed. One group even took a solemn oath, in the name of God, that they would give their "life, liberty, influence" and all else "for the destruction of Joseph Smith and his party."

During a conference meeting held in Nauvoo in the spring of 1843, an officer came to arrest Joseph Smith the Prophet; but in order to prevent him from doing so, a number of boys, including myself, commenced whittling sticks and whistling and every time the officer neared the house where the Prophet was, we would stand in front of him and whittle and whistle. The result of this was that he did not arrest Joseph Smith that day."

—SAMUEL WOOLLEY

A few months before his death, Joseph bestowed a fulness of the priesthood keys on the members of the Quorum of the Twelve Apostles.

With his enemies pressing close, Joseph knew that he might be killed. He also knew that the Lord's work must go on. Therefore, a few months before his death, he gave the Twelve the temple endowment. Then, "when they received their endowment," Wilford Woodruff recorded, they "actually received the keys of the kingdom of God." On that occasion, Joseph exclaimed, "Upon your shoulders the kingdom rests, and you must round up your shoulders, and bear it; for I have had to do it until now. But now the responsibility rests upon you. It mattereth not what becomes of me."

Curtis Edwin Bolton wrote: "The last I saw of Joseph Smith he was standing with his youngest boy in the middle of the street. No one was near him. He was a most beautiful formed man, and was laughing pleasantly to the brethren on board the steamboat—who were leaving to go a preaching—I never in this life shall look upon his like again."

MARTYRDOM OF THE PROPHET

The enemies of the Prophet in Nauvoo grew increasingly dangerous. On more than one occasion Joseph had to hide or flee to evade those who would do him harm.

Hyrum stood by his brother through it all. Joseph feared that if his own life were taken, Hyrum's would be taken as well. At one point Joseph wrote: "Brother Hyrum, what a faithful heart you have got! Oh may the Eternal Jehovah crown eternal blessing upon your head, as a reward for the care you have had for my soul! O how many are the sorrows we have shared together. . . . Hyrum, thy name shall be written in the book of the law of the Lord, for those who come after thee to look upon, that they may pattern after thy works."

On more than one occasion, Joseph had to hide or flee from his enemies. Hyrum was often at his side.

In an attempt to flee their enemies, Joseph and Hyrum escaped across the Mississippi River.

As time passed, old enemies from Missouri began to gather around Nauvoo. Joseph appealed to the governor of Illinois for help. At first the governor seemed willing, but then he sent a letter that was uncooperative and demanding.

When Joseph read the letter, he said, "There is no mercy—no mercy here." Hyrum replied, "No, just as sure as we fall into their hands we are dead men." Joseph looked to his older brother Hyrum for counsel. "What shall we do, Brother Hyrum?" Hyrum wasn't sure. "I don't know."

Then Joseph's face lit up, and he said: "The way is open. It is clear to my mind what to do. All they want is Hyrum and myself; then tell everybody to go about their business, and not to collect in groups, but to scatter about. . . . They will not harm you in person or property, and not even a hair of your head. We will cross the river tonight, and go away to the west."

After bidding farewell to their families and making arrangements for their temporary care, Joseph, Hyrum, and Willard Richards were rowed across the Mississippi River in a leaky skiff by Orrin Porter Rockwell. After they arrived on the west bank, they asked Rockwell to go back to Nauvoo to gather animals and supplies they could take with them as they fled to the Great Basin in the Rocky Mountains.

> I told Stephen Markham that if I and Hyrum were ever taken again we should be massacred, or I was not a prophet of God. I want Hyrum to live to avenge my blood, but he is determined not to leave me."
>
> —JOSEPH SMITH, THE LAST ENTRY IN HIS JOURNAL

Fourteen-year-old Eunice Billings remembered: "On the last day which he spent in Nauvoo, he passed our house with his brother Hyrum, both riding. My mother and I were standing in the dooryard, and as he passed he bowed with uplifted hat to my mother. Hyrum seemed like one in a dream, sad and despondent, taking no notice of anyone. They were on their way to the Carthage jail, and it was the last time I saw the Prophet alive."

Early in the morning of June 23, 1844, a posse arrived in Nauvoo to arrest Joseph. When they didn't find him, they returned to Carthage. That same afternoon, Emma sent Orrin Porter Rockwell back to Joseph, accompanied by Reynolds Cahoon. They carried a letter from Emma begging him to return. Reynolds Cahoon and others accused Joseph of cowardice for wanting to leave the people to the mobs and the troops. They compared him to the fable of the shepherd who, when the wolves came, ran from his flock and left the sheep to be devoured.

Downcast, Joseph replied, "If my life is of no value to my friends it is of none to myself." He turned to his friend Porter Rockwell. "What shall I do?"

Rockwell replied, "You . . . ought to know best; and as you make your bed, I will lie with you."

Joseph then asked Hyrum, "Brother Hyrum, you are the oldest, what shall we do?"

Hyrum said, "Let us go back and give ourselves up, and see the thing out."

Joseph paused a few moments in deep thought and then he said, "If you go back I will go with you, but we shall be butchered."

Joseph and the others crossed the river back to Nauvoo, intending to go to Carthage to face their accusers. As Joseph rode his horse slowly past the homes and businesses of Nauvoo, then past the temple on the hill, he paused. "This is the loveliest place and the best people under the heavens," he said. "Little do they know the trials that await them."

Lewis Barney wrote: "Some of the Brethren was in favor of having him go to Carthage and stand his trial and said it would all come out right and he would be acquitted and that would put an end to the trouble. I told them that if Brother Joseph ever went to Carthage he would never get away alive. I lived in the neighborhood of Carthage about 3 miles from town and knew their intense, wicked hatred against Joseph and the Mormons, and that it was their intention to get him there and assassinate him."

As they made their final journey to Carthage, Joseph, Hyrum, and others rode past the unfinished Nauvoo Temple.

John Taylor sang to the Prophet and others in Carthage Jail.

As Joseph departed Nauvoo to go to Carthage, he said: "I am going like a lamb to the slaughter, but I am calm as a summer's morning. I have a conscience void of offense toward God and toward all men. If they take my life I shall die an innocent man."

When Joseph and Hyrum arrived in Carthage, they were charged with treason and were imprisoned in Carthage Jail. With them were a number of other brethren, but some were later released. In the end, only John Taylor and Willard Richards remained with them.

The prisoners were held for two days. Then, on the third day, they began to feel increasingly depressed. John Taylor, who had a fine singing voice, sang "A Poor Wayfaring Man of Grief" for them. Joseph asked him to sing the song again, but John said he didn't feel like singing anymore. But when Hyrum encouraged him, John sang the entire song—all seven verses—again.

Late in the afternoon of June 27, 1844, they heard gunshots and looked out the window. Below them were more than a hundred men with their faces painted black. The men stormed the jail, bullets flying. Hyrum was shot in the face and the back. He fell dead to the floor. John Taylor was shot in many places, but he survived. Willard Richards was unharmed.

And Joseph was hit by the window. He fell through the window to the ground. Joseph Smith, the prophet of God, was dead.

John Taylor sang one of Joseph's favorite hymns, "A Poor Wayfaring Man of Grief," in Carthage Jail:

A poor wayfaring Man of grief
Hath often crossed me on my way,
Who sued so humbly for relief
That I could never answer nay.
I had not pow'r to ask his name,
Whereto he went, or whence he came;
Yet there was something in his eye
That won my love; I knew not why. . . .

In pris'n I saw him next, condemned
To meet a traitor's doom at morn.
The tide of lying tongues I stemmed,
And honored him 'mid shame and scorn.
My friendship's utmost zeal to try,
He asked if I for him would die.
The flesh was weak; my blood ran chill,
But my free spirit cried, "I will!"

Then in a moment to my view
The stranger started from disguise.
The tokens in his hands I knew;
The Savior stood before mine eyes.
He spake, and my poor name he named,
"Of me thou hast not been ashamed.
These deeds shall thy memorial be;
Fear not, thou didst them unto me."

When they heard the news, the Saints were heartbroken. Many both inside and outside the Church expected that it would die with the Prophet gone. But it has lived on, directed and sustained by the power of God. Other prophets have followed, and the Church has continued to fulfill its divinely ordained purpose on the earth. Saints around the world express undying gratitude to Joseph Smith, the founding prophet of this dispensation, and to Jesus Christ, who called that prophet and who directs the affairs of the Church.

"They lived for glory; they died for glory; and glory is their eternal reward."

After the martyrdom of Joseph and Hyrum Smith, John Taylor recorded a testimony that still speaks to us today: "The testators are now dead, and their testament is in force. . . . Henceforward their names will be classed among the martyrs of religion; and the reader in every nation will be reminded that the Book of Mormon, and this book of Doctrine and Covenants of the church, cost the best blood of the nineteenth century to bring them forth for the salvation of a ruined world. . . . They lived for glory; they died for glory; and glory is their eternal reward" (D&C 135:4–5).

William W. Phelps, a close associate of Joseph and Hyrum, wrote a poem that he read at their funeral, which has since been turned into a favorite Latter-day Saint hymn:

Praise to the man who communed with Jehovah!
Jesus anointed that Prophet and Seer.
Blessed to open the last dispensation,
Kings shall extol him, and nations revere.

Praise to his mem'ry, he died as a martyr;
Honored and blest be his ever great name!
Long shall his blood, which was shed by assassins,
Plead unto heav'n while the earth lauds his fame. . . .

Sacrifice brings forth the blessings of heaven;
Earth must atone for the blood of that man.
Wake up the world for the conflict of justice.
Millions shall know "Brother Joseph" again.

Hail to the Prophet, ascended to heaven!
Traitors and tyrants now fight him in vain.
Mingling with Gods, he can plan for his brethren;
Death cannot conquer the hero again.

SOURCES

page 2: Joseph Fielding Smith, *Church History and Modern Revelation* (1953), 1:4.

page 3: Lucy Mack Smith, *History of Joseph Smith by His Mother* (1996), 73.

page 4: Smith, *History of Joseph Smith*, 86.

page 6: Smith, *History of Joseph Smith*, 86.

page 9: Joseph Smith—History 1:5, 10–12.

page 10: Joseph Smith—History 1:13–20.

page 12: Joseph F. Smith, *Gospel Doctrine* (1939), 488; Joseph Smith—History 1:21–25.

page 14: Joseph Smith—History 1:28, 55; "Stories from Notebook of Martha Cox, Grandmother of Fern Cox Anderson," typescript, LDS Church Archives, Salt Lake City, Utah.

page 17: Joseph Smith—History 1:30, 32–33, 44, 49–50.

page 19: Joseph Smith—History 1:50, 52–53, 57; Smith, *History of Joseph Smith*, 87, 111; William Smith, *Deseret Evening News*, 20 January 1891.

page 23: Joseph Smith, *History of the Church*, 7 vols. (1948–50), 4:537.

page 25: Smith, *History of Joseph Smith*, 163, 165–66.

page 26: Joseph Smith—History, 1:71 note.

page 28: Joseph Smith—History 1:68–73.

page 30: Smith, *History of the Church*, 1:54–55; Smith, *History of Joseph Smith*, 199.

page 31: Smith, *History of the Church*, 1:66, 84.

page 32: Smith, *History of the Church*, 1:77–79; Smith, *History of Joseph Smith*, 223.

page 34: Parley P. Pratt, *Autobiography of Parley P. Pratt* (1985), 40.

page 35: Edward W. Tullidge, *The Women of Mormondom* (1877), 41–42; Orson F. Whitney, in Conference Report, April 1912, 50.

page 37: Elizabeth Ann Whitney, *Woman's Exponent* 7 (1878): 51.

page 40: Wilford Woodruff, quoted in Conference Report, April 1898, 57; Smith, *History of Joseph Smith*, 322.

page 43: Pratt, *Autobiography of Parley P. Pratt*, 75; Margaret Pierce Young, journal excerpts, typescript, LDS Church Archives, Salt Lake City, Utah, 1–3.

page 44: Smith, *History of the Church*, 2:428.

page 46: Matthias F. Cowley, *Wilford Woodruff: His Life and Labors* (1964), 29; Smith, *History of the Church*, 2:378–79.

page 47: Levi Jackman, "A Short Sketch of the Life of Levi Jackman," typescript, Harold B. Lee Library, Brigham Young University, 4.

page 49: Pratt, *Autobiography of Parley P. Pratt*, 82, 83.

page 51: Joseph Bates Noble, "Autobiography of Joseph Bates Noble," typescript, Harold B. Lee Library, Brigham Young University, 5–7.

page 52: Smith, *History of the Church*, 2:489–90; David Osborn, *Juvenile Instructor* 27 (1892): 173.

page 53: Joseph Holbrook, "Autobiography (1806–1846)," typescript, Harold B. Lee Library, Brigham Young University, 44.

page 54: Smith, *History of the Church*, 3:175; emphasis in original; Gordon B. Hinckley, *Ensign*, May 1980, 61.

page 56: John W. Hess, *Juvenile Instructor* 27 (1892): 302.

page 59: Dimick Huntington, quoted in David E. and Della S. Miller, *Nauvoo: The City of Joseph* (1974), 26; spelling and punctuation modernized.

page 60: "A Sketch of the Life of Eunice Billings Snow," *Woman's Exponent* 39 (1910): 14; Calvin W. Moore, *Juvenile Instructor* 27 (1892): 255.

page 61: Journal of Wandle Mace, typescript, Harold B. Lee Library, Brigham Young University, 101.

page 62: Lucy M. Smith, "Recollections of the Prophet Joseph Smith," *Juvenile Instructor* 27 (1892): 470; Smith, *History of the Church*, 5:307.

page 64: Edwin Holdman, *Juvenile Instructor* 27 (1892): 153.

page 65: *Juvenile Instructor* 27 (1892): 399–400; *Woman's Exponent* 12 (1883): 51; Smith, *History of the Church*, 567–68.

page 66: Emma Smith Papers, 1 August 1868 or 1869, 4.

page 67: Smith, *History of the Church*, 6:364; *Contributor* 5 (April 1884): 255; Preston W. Parkinson, *The Utah Woolley Family* (Salt Lake City, 1967).

page 69: *Times and Seasons*, 5:698; Curtis Edward Bolton, *Reminiscences and Journal*, LDS Church Archives.

page 70: Smith, *History of the Church*, 5:107–8.

page 71: Smith, *History of the Church*, 6:545–46.

page 72: Smith, *History of the Church*, 6:548–50; 554; *Woman's Exponent* 39 (August 1910): 14; *Autobiography of Lewis Barney*, paragraph 69.

page 75: Smith, *History of the Church*, 6:555; *Hymns of The Church of Jesus Christ of Latter-day Saints*, no. 29.

page 76: *Hymns*, no. 27.

ACKNOWLEDGMENTS

"Blessed be the name of our God; let us sing to his praise, yea, let us give thanks to his holy name, for he doth work righteousness forever."—Alma 26:8

I appreciate the support and inspiration that I receive from my wife, Pamela. I love it when I'm about to start another painting and she says, "Do you think you ought to finish something?" Or better yet, when I show her a painting that I have finally finished and she says, "That painting is really going to be nice when it's finished!" Even though she thinks I'm a good painter, she helps me stay grounded.

Thanks to my children, Travis, Heather, Todd, Summer, and Holly, all opinionated adults now, for their encouragement and moral support. Thanks, Todd, for the computer tech support.

I am grateful to the people at Deseret Book who patiently kept me at it. Jana Erickson directed this project. Jay Parry edited my manuscript, and Shauna Gibby designed this beautiful book. Laurie Cook did the typography. Whenever I wanted to go to Salt Lake and stick my nose into things, they made me stay home and paint, and they made it seem like my idea.

I owe a debt of gratitude to those people who lived during the time of the restoration of the gospel, who met Joseph Smith and shared their thoughts and feelings about him.

I tip my hat in thanks to three artists who painted during Joseph Smith's lifetime: William Sydney Mount, Francis Edmonds, and George Caleb Bingham, all of whom painted scenes of "just plain old Americans." They are important resources for anyone interested in depicting the "Restoration" period of Church history.

I can't say enough about my friend Carma De Jong Anderson, who is a true expert in early nineteenth-century clothing and lifestyle. Carma comes right to the point when she tells artists that something is wrong in their painting, film, or historical display. I love that she is a straight shooter, and though she has ruffled a lot of feathers, she is ever generous and willing to share her vast knowledge of Victorian and pre-Victorian dress and manners.

And of course, thanks to Joseph Smith for the life he lived. To me he has become a great friend. I hope these pages give you a peek into the life and times of the Prophet Joseph Smith.